WRITTEN IN RED

The Story of a Savior

by

Wendy F. McMillian

Word of His Mouth Publishers
Mooresboro, NC

All Scripture quotations are taken from the **King James Version** of the Bible.

ISBN: 978-0-9856042-5-7
Printed in the United States of America
©2012 Wendy F. McMillian

Word of His Mouth Publishers
PO Box 256
Mooresboro, NC 28114
704-477-5439
www.wordofhismouth.com

Table of Content

Introduction

Most of us remember the horror of September 11, 2001, when jet airplanes were crashed into the twin towers in New York and the Pentagon. Most of us even remember the heroics of those aboard the other plane that was directed toward destroying other landmarks and places in the U.S. The men and women aboard that plane knew they were going to die because of the pilot's hatred toward Americans. They knew that they were destined to become part of a mass suicide run. So, in an effort to save those they loved and to save other fellow Americans, they overtook the pilot and crashed the plane where no one would be injured or killed apart from those aboard the plane. Those brave men and women sacrificed their life that others might live. But these men and women sacrificed their life for just a few.

I once read another story about a single man who sacrificed His life. This man was beaten beyond recognition, was laughed and sneered at and was paraded down busy streets before being put to death. His death was agonizing and excruciating. This story is one of a devoted Savior, a love story only found in the Holy Bible. Why call it a love story if the Man's death was so brutal? It is a love story because the Man who died, died for me. He died that I might live. He sacrificed Himself for me, to forgive me of my sins. What greater love can someone show to another than giving their life for them? "Greater love hath no man than this, that a man lay down his life for his friends." (John 15:13). What kind of a Man would do such a thing? His name is Jesus.

This man, Jesus, not only died for me but also for all of mankind as well. Most of us would probably lay down our life for our loved ones, ones that are truly close to our heart, ones that we know truly love us in return. But, not many of us would suffer an agonizing punishment and death for total strangers. Jesus freely gave His life as a sacrifice for all. "Therefore doth my Father love me, because *I lay down my life*, that I might take it again," (**bold** and *italic* emphasis mine, John 10:17). He died for the entire world. He died for you. He died for people that hated Him and despised Him, who hate and despise Him still. His sole mission while here on earth was to meet this violent death. Why would someone's mission be to meet death? He died that He might redeem mankind. His love surpasses any love found here on earth. His love is never ending and ever forgiving.

Through the pages of this book, this great love is explored. It is my hope that those who do not know this Man Jesus will read this book and accept Him as their personal Savior. And that those who already know Him as their Savior will have a closer relationship with Him. It is also my hope that all will come to appreciate this great love sent down to us.

I would like to tell you the story of this Precious Savior.

Chapter 1
A Name Above Every Name

Proper introductions must come first in order to truly relate to someone. The man I call Savior is referred to in many different ways in the Bible. Isaiah called Him, "Wonderful, Counsellor, The mighty God, The everlasting Father, The Prince of Peace," (Isaiah 9:6b). Peter called Him the "chief Shepherd" (I Peter 5:4). John the Baptist called Him, "the Lamb of God, which taketh away the sin of the world," (John 1:29). Paul called Him "Potentate, the King of Kings, and Lord of lords," (I Timothy 6:15). He is described as being the Light of the world (John 9:5), "the Judge of the quick and dead," (Acts 10:42), the "heir of all things," (Hebrews 1:2). He carries the title of "Alpha and Omega, the first and the last" (Revelation 1:11). But He is best known as The Lord Jesus Christ.

You could say that this title is His full name. Just as we are usually given a first, middle and last name by our birth parents, Jesus was also given a first, middle and last name. Names have meaning. The title Lord distinguishes Jesus as a King over all kings. It is most always capitalized in Scripture and indicates that Jesus is the One Lord over all. The name of Jesus is a special name, like our first names by which we are called. The name of Jesus occurs over 900 times in Scripture. It is derived from the Hebrew Yeshua or Joshua and means "Salvation," or "the Lord is salvation," or "the Lord Saves," (Christian Answers.net, 1995-2012). It reveals that Jesus is the Redeemer of mankind. The name of Christ translates into Messiah or Anointed One. ChristianAnswers.net defines it this way:

> "To believe that 'Jesus is the Christ' is to believe that he is the Anointed, the Messiah of the prophets, the Savior sent of God, that he was, in a word, what he claimed to be. This is to believe the gospel, by the faith of which alone men can be brought unto God. That Jesus is the Christ is the testimony of God, and the faith of this constitutes a Christian (I Corinthians 12:3, I John 5:1),"

(ChristianAnswers.net, 1995-2012).

The word "the" before the Savior's name should not be dismissed. "The" is a definite article that is used "for emphasis before titles and names or to suggest uniqueness often" (Merriam-Webster Dictionary, 2012). The use of the word "the" before Jesus' name and title points to His uniqueness as both God and man.

The birth of Jesus was predicted in Isaiah 7:14b when God said, "Behold a virgin shall conceive, and bear a son, and shall call his name Immanuel." The prophecy came to life when Joseph, the husband of Mary, was told, "fear not to take unto thee Mary thy wife: for that which is conceived in her is of the Holy Ghost. And she shall bring forth a son, and thou shalt call his name JESUS: for he shall save his people from their sins," (Matthew 1:20b-21). "Now all this was done, that it might be fulfilled which was spoken of the Lord by the prophet, saying, Behold, a virgin shall be with child, and shall bring forth a son, and they shall call his name Emmanuel," (Matthew 1:22-23a). The name Immanuel, whether spelled with an "I" or an "E" means "God with us" (Rose Publishing, 2006). "And he shall pass through Judah; ... O Immanuel. ... for God is with us," (Isaiah 8:8a and 8:10b). "And they shall call his name Emmanuel, which being interpreted is, God with us," (Matthew 1:23b). The name Immanuel denotes that Jesus was God incarnate or God personified.

God was indeed with mankind when He appeared in human form as Jesus. The name Jesus signifies a Savior, "for he shall save his people from their sins" (Matthew 1:21b). A Savior, of course, is someone who redeems or rescues another. Jesus is our Redeemer from our sins against God. Jesus is also referred to as Christ, "And Jacob begat Joseph the husband of Mary, of whom was born Jesus, who is called Christ," (Matthew 1:16). The name of Christ is mentioned over 500 times in the Bible, beginning in the Gospel of Matthew and ending in the book of the Revelation.

Jesus was given a special name because of His special purpose. His sole purpose was to become a sinless sacrifice for mankind. "To this end was I born, and for this cause came I into the world, that I should bear witness unto the truth," (John 18:37b). "For to this end Christ both died, and rose, and revived, that he might be Lord both of the dead and living," (Romans 14:9). "But God commendeth his love toward us, in that, while we were yet sinners, Christ died for us," (Romans 5:8). Thus, the name of The Lord Jesus Christ was unique and special. "Wherefore God also hath highly exalted him, and given him a name which is above every name," (Philippians 2:9).

What kind of love does it take to become a sacrifice for all humanity? To even begin to understand this ultimate, sacrificial love, you must uncover the depths of Christ's love. His love for us is immeasurable, infinite, and boundless, and yet the Bible tells us of it in great detail.

Chapter 2
God's Four-Dimensional Love

Love is defined as having "a strong affection for another arising out of kinship or personal ties" (Merriam-Webster, 2012). Love is mentioned over 400 times in the Bible. There are different types of love. You love your spouse in a much different way than you love your children. You love your children differently than you love your pets. You love your friends differently than you love a family member or boyfriend or girlfriend. A parent loves a child because they are kin to one another. A husband loves his wife because they are partners and share a special connection. A person loves a friend because they are a companion. Love appears in many forms.

When someone accepts Christ as their personal Savior, they immediately become an adopted member of the family of God. Ephesians 1:5 says, "Having predestinated us unto the adoption of children by Jesus Christ to himself, according to the good pleasure of his will." God adopted us into His family through His Son, Jesus. By being adopted through Jesus, we have a special kinship, a personal tie or bond with the Most High God. The Scripture says that it was God's good pleasure and His will for us to become His sons and daughters through His Son, Christ Jesus. What a wonderful and exciting thought this is!

How is it possible to become the sons and daughters of God? After all, God did create us, are we not already His? John's Gospel will help shed some light on this. Jesus told Nicodemus that, "Except a man be born again, he cannot see the kingdom of God," (John 3:3b). Nicodemus was a well-educated Pharisee and devout Jew. When Jesus told him that he must be born again, he replied, "How can a man be born when he is old? Can he enter the second time into his mother's womb, and be born?" (John 3:4b). Good question! How can anyone be born a second time? Nicodemus was puzzled at what Jesus said to him. However, Jesus was not speaking of a literal rebirthing from his natural mother. He explained to Nicodemus, "Except a man be born of water and of the Spirit, he cannot enter into the kingdom of God," (John 3:5). Jesus made it plain that mankind must experience two births – one *physical* and one *spiritual*. All of us experience the first birth that Jesus mentions, the **physical** birthing from our mother's womb. The second birthing, on the other hand, is a **spiritual** birthing that can only come through Jesus Christ. This spiritual birthing earns us the right to be called the sons and daughters of God.

When Adam and Eve were first created, they were sinless and innocent. Nevertheless, sin entered into the world because of Adam, and fellowship with God was broken. God could no longer walk and talk with Adam in the garden as He had done before (refer to Genesis 3:8). Adam and Eve both suffered a spiritual death through this loss of fellowship.

In order for that fellowship to be restored to mankind, a mediator or a "go between" had to bridge the gap that was made between God and mankind. Mankind needed someone to re-establish his fellowship with God. That mediator had to be sinless and without any offense in order to speak to or present Himself before God Almighty. The mediator also had to be able to communicate with mankind as well as with God. That mediator was Jesus. (All these things will be further explained in chapters four and five.) Jesus returned our fellowship with God by becoming a sinless sacrifice and payment for our sins in the form of a man.

However, we must first realize that we are sinners and then we must ask Jesus to forgive us in order for fellowship to be restored. Jesus provides the way, but we must accept His payment. When we receive forgiveness, we encounter a *spiritual rebirthing*. Our communion with God is restored. "But as many as received him (Jesus), to them gave he power to become the sons of God, even to them that believe on his name; **Which were born**, not of blood, nor of the will of the flesh, nor of the will of man, but **of God.**" The key words here are – which were born … of God. (**bold** emphasis and input mine, John 1:12-3) We are spiritually reborn upon accepting Christ as Savior, and we are adopted as sons and daughters!

Now Jesus warns, "Marvel not that I said unto thee, Ye must be born again. The wind bloweth where it listeth, and thou hearest the sound thereof, but canst not tell whence it cometh, and whither it goeth: so is every one that is born of the Spirit." (John 3:7, 8) Jesus said not to wonder, doubt, question, or be amazed that He said we must be born again. Jesus said just as you believe in the wind that you cannot physically see but know that it blows through the trees, you must believe by faith that Jesus saves from sin and provides that spiritual rebirthing needed to communicate with God.

Why would such a sovereign God choose us to be His sons and daughters? We have done nothing worthy of His attention. We have no special power or ability of our own. Since the beginning of time, we have rejected and refused God by taking Him out of our homes and our churches, out of our children and our justice system. We are imperfect beings. Yet, He chose us. Why? He chose us because of His love for us. Ephesians 2:4 tells us, "But God, who is rich in mercy, for **his great love** wherewith he loved us" (**bold** emphasis mine). He could hate us because we have abandoned Him but He chooses to love us. His great love toward us is nothing short of mind-boggling.

How could God love such wicked, vile people as we are? First John 4:8 and 16 tells us why, "He that loveth not knoweth not God; **for *God is love*. And we have known and believed the love that God hath to us. *God is love*; and he that dwelleth in love dwelleth in God, and God in him," (*Italic* and **bold** emphasis mine). God **is** love. The greatest love story ever written to mankind is found within the pages of the Holy Bible. In every book, every chapter, and every verse, the great love of God is exposed.

God's love is not one-sided as ours sometimes is. Often times we love only those who love us in return. On the other hand, we may only love those who are of a certain race, sex, or creed. Maybe we love only those that have the same personality as ours. Sometimes we love one person more than another person. Unlike us, we are told that God does not show favoritism or prejudice concerning mankind. Romans 2:11 says, "For there is no respect of persons with God." We are His children and He loves us, no matter our color, race, sex, personality, or creed.

The Bible tells us in Ephesians 3:16-19, "That he would grant you, according to the riches of his glory, to be strengthened with might by his Spirit in the inner man; That Christ may dwell in your hearts by faith; that ye, being rooted and grounded in love, May be able to comprehend with all saints what is **the breadth, and length, and depth, and height**; And to know the love of Christ, which passeth knowledge, that ye might be filled with all the fullness of God" (**bold** emphasis mine). Ephesians brings to light that there are four sides to the love of Christ, making it 4-dimensional – having breadth, length, depth and height. The word "dimension" means "measured out." Christ's love is measured out in these verses in Ephesians. There are four Gospels in the Bible - Matthew, Mark, Luke, and John. There are four seasons – spring, summer, fall, and winter. There are four corners of the earth - North, South, East, and West. The number four in the Bible represents all of God's creation. It represents the world. Since the love of Christ is 4-dimensional, we know that it covers the entire world. "And this gospel of the kingdom shall be preached in all the world for a witness unto all nations; and then shall the end come," (Matthew 24:14; also read Luke 11:50 and John 12:47). Nevertheless, to truly appreciate and comprehend the completeness of the love of Christ, each dimension deserves its own exploration.

Chapter 3
The Breadth of God's Love

The first dimension of God's love mentioned in Ephesians 3:18 is **breadth**. John 3:16 tells us, "For God so loved the world, that he gave his only begotten son, that whosoever believeth in him should not perish, but have everlasting life." So often this verse is memorized and recited without any emotion or feeling. This is probably the single most powerful verse in the entire Word of God. No other verse in the Bible can explain God's love for mankind as clearly as John 3:16. Let us consider a few words – often overlooked – from this verse.

One of the smallest words in John 3:16 is the little word *so*. This little word, even though small, packs a powerful punch. "Dynamite comes in small packages" as the old saying goes. The little word "so" is a small package of dynamite. Its definition is, "to a great extent" (Merriam-Webster, 2012). Think of the many ways in which you have used this little word. "I love you **so** much." "We are **so** blessed." The use of *so* in these sentences makes them seem stronger and adds more meaning to the entire sentence. It serves the same purpose in John 3:16. Put the definition of so into this verse and it reads, "For God [to a great extent] loved the world." The word extent means size. Imagine the size of God's love toward us in that He would love all nations, all races, and all creeds of people. There are over six billion people living on Earth. Just think of all the gravesites you have seen in your neighborhood or local towns. There are probably more people in the grave than there are living. God loves each and every one of them. That is a broad love. Our love pales in comparison to God's love toward mankind.

One word that is sometimes left out, dismissed, or even overlooked in John 3:16 is the word begotten. Dismissal or removal of this word causes a change in the whole idea and meaning of the verse. Begotten comes from the word beget, which means, "to procreate as the father" (Merriam-Webster, 2012). The word "procreate" means "bring forth" (Merriam-Webster, 2012). This word is very important because it tells of Jesus' birthright, His patrimony, and His heritage. God **brought forth** His Son Jesus.

God created two bodies for two sons, Adam and Jesus. Genesis 2:7 tells us, "And the Lord God formed man of the dust of the ground, and breathed into his nostrils the breath of life; and man became a living soul." Adam was not born of a woman but was created from the dust of the ground. He was not conceived from the union of a man and a woman. God formed Adam's body out of the dust of the Earth then breathed the breath of life into him. This was the first beginnings of mankind.

God the Father also created the physical body of His Son, Jesus. Jesus was conceived from the Holy Spirit of God, which is of the Holy Trinity. "But while he thought on these things, behold, the angel of the Lord appeared unto him in a dream, saying, Joseph, thou son of David, fear not to take unto thee Mary thy wife: **for that which is conceived in her is of the Holy Ghost**," (**bold** emphasis mine, Matthew 1:20). Consider the three-leaf clover that has three petals that make up the clover. Three leaves reside on one stem making the clover. Consider also our physical makeup as human beings. We have a body, soul, and spirit, each of which is different from the other. Like the clover and our physical form, God has three parts to His being – God the Father, God the Son, and God the Holy Spirit. Three entities reside as One Being.

The Holy Spirit is God in Spirit form, "God is a Spirit: and they that worship him must worship him in spirit and in truth," (John 4:24). Jesus was God in human form, "Believest thou not that I am **in the Father**, and the **Father in me**? the words that I speak unto you I speak not of myself: but the **Father that dwelleth in me**, he doeth the works," (**bold** emphasis mine, (John 14:10). "And the **Word was made flesh**, and dwelt among us, (and we beheld his glory, the glory as of **the only begotten of the Father**,) full of grace and truth," (**bold** emphasis mine, John 1:14). God is the Father **and** Creator **and** Head of all three, "In the beginning **God** created the heaven and the earth," (Gen. 1:1). God, in His Trinity, has always existed.

Jesus was made flesh but His Father was not an earthly one. Jesus was conceived of God. "And, behold, thou shalt conceive in thy womb, and bring forth a son, and shalt call his name JESUS. Then said Mary unto the angel, How shall this be, seeing I know not a man? And the angel answered and said unto her, The Holy Ghost shall come upon thee, and the power of the Highest shall overshadow thee: therefore also that holy thing which shall be born of thee shall be called the Son of God," (Luke 1:31, 34, 35). Jesus' *conception* was a Holy conception. God impregnated Mary by the Holy Ghost. In studying a little science here, we know that a baby inherits chromosomes from both its mother **and its father**. Chromosomes are the rod-shaped or threadlike DNA-containing structures that house genes – which give the baby its characteristics and traits. Knowing this, we know that Jesus had the traits of His Father, God.

Jesus was born as all human beings after Adam and Eve were born. He was born out of His mother's womb. "And she brought forth her firstborn son, and wrapped him in swaddling clothes, and laid him in a manger; because there was no room for them in the inn," (Luke 2:7). Because of Jesus' conception from God (His Father) and being born of a virgin (His mother), His *birth* was a holy birth. "Therefore the Lord himself shall give you a sign; Behold, **a virgin shall conceive**, and bear a son, and shall call his name Immanuel," (**bold** emphasis mine, Isaiah 7:14) "Behold, **a virgin** shall be with child, and shall bring forth a son, and they shall call his name Emmanuel, which being interpreted is, God with us," (**bold** emphasis mine, Matt. 1:23). Jesus is the only Son that was both brought forth from the seed of God *and* born of a woman. Jesus was begotten of God. The word begotten must not be removed or changed in John 3:16.

The next word to consider is whosoever. Whosoever means "whatever person" (Merriam-Webster, 2012). Look up the definition of whatever and you will find it means "anything or everything, no matter what" (Merriam-Webster, 2012). Now consider these definitions in the verse "[that

any person, no matter what], believeth in him".
I have heard many sinners say that they have
done too much evil to be redeemed or forgiven
of Jesus. God tells us here that all are welcome
– no stipulations or conditions have to be met.
Remember – anything, no matter what. No
matter what evil you have done, no matter if
mankind does not forgive you, no matter if
you do not forgive yourself, God will forgive
you of all things, if you will only repent to
Him. What a wonderful Savior we have!

In continuing our exploration of John
3:16, we find another word to reflect on is
"perish." Perish means, "to become destroyed
or die" (Merriam-Webster, 2012). In Hebrews
9:27 we are told that we all have an
appointment with death, "For it is appointed
unto man once to die." This should not be our
greatest concern, nor should we let this part of
the verse worry us. Death is inevitable. We
will all die someday, somehow. Our concern
should be focused rather on the second part of
this verse which says, "but after this the
judgment." We are told that judgment is
coming. It is at this judgment that our fate will
be revealed, a fate that will be for all eternity.
If we have accepted Jesus as our Savior and
have been redeemed through His blood,
Heaven will be our eternal home. If we have
rejected Him and have not accepted Him as
Savior, Hell will be our eternal home.

The Bible speaks of two very different
deaths. The first death is a physical death, a

death of the body. As said earlier, Hebrews 9:27 tells us that this death is an appointment that all mankind must meet; therefore, we need not fret or worry over this death because it will come. The other death spoken of in the Bible is the Second Death. This death represents the total and complete separation from God and His kingdom for all eternity. It is a spiritual death. You might ask, "Who is going to this Second Death?" Revelation 21:8 tells us who - "But the fearful, and unbelieving, and the abominable, and murderers, and whoremongers, and sorcerers, and idolaters, and all liars, shall have their part in the lake which burneth with fire and brimstone: which is the second death." Here we are told that those who did not believe or trust (unbelieving) that Jesus Christ could save them from their sins, those who were too afraid (fearful) to accept Him as their Savior and those that never asked Jesus to forgive them of their sins but chose rather to live in them (abominable), will be cast into a lake of fire and brimstone. What a sad day this will be for many. Our loved ones, friends, neighbors and coworkers may be among those cast into this lake of fire, forever separated from God.

The Bible tells us in II Peter 3:9 that "The Lord is not slack concerning his promise, as some men count slackness; but is longsuffering to us-ward, **not willing that any should perish**, but that all should come to repentance," (**bold** emphasis mine). This is why Jesus died upon the cross. Jesus Himself tells us in John 18:37, "To this end was I born, and for this cause came I into the world, that I should bear witness unto the truth." He was offered as a sacrifice for our sins, "That whosoever believeth in Him should not perish." If we believe these things and trust Jesus to redeem us from this Second Death, we can escape an eternal home in Hell. We must simply believe in Jesus' power to redeem us from this Second Death.

The last part of John 3:16 tells us that we will be granted everlasting life if we only believe in Jesus' ability to redeem us from our sins. What is everlasting life? Everlasting means "eternal, lasting or enduring through all time" (Merriam-Webster, 2012). God wants us to have [eternal, lasting through all time], life. We do not have to suffer the spiritual death and separation from God because of the Second Death; we have the choice to live eternally in Heaven with Jesus.

By putting all these definitions into John 3:16 (not for the purpose of altering or changing God's Word), you will see how truly powerful a verse this is.

> For God [to a great extent] loved the world that he gave His only [brought forth Son], that [any person, no matter what], believeth in him should not [die or be destroyed], but

have [eternal, lasting through all time] life. <u>What power!</u>

Another way to look at John 3:16 is:

God (the Greatest Lover)
so loved (to the greatest degree)
the world (the greatest company)
that He gave (the greatest act)
His only begotten Son (the greatest gift)
that whosoever (the greatest opportunity)
believeth (the greatest simplicity)
in Him (the greatest attraction)
should not perish (the greatest promise)
but (the greatest difference)
have (the greatest certainty)
everlasting life (the greatest possession)

This is the width or broadness of God's wonderful love toward us. There is no boundary, it is not for certain people, but it is for everyone that is willing to accept it. It is a free gift that wraps around the world – reaching every man, woman and child no matter their race, religion or nationality. The love of God is so broad that it reaches around the entire globe.

Chapter 4
The Length of God's Love

Objects are considered to be 3-dimensional when they have depth, width and height (such as a cube). In Ephesians 3:18, we are told that God's love not only has width (or breadth), depth and height but it also has a fourth dimension – **length**. Basically, there are 4-dimensions that we are aware of as humans. Free math lesson here! They are a point (Zeroth (0) dimension), a line (1st – dimension), a square (2nd – dimension), a cube (3rd – dimension) and a tesseract (4th – dimension, sometimes – and in this case will be – referred to as time). By this classification, Ephesians 3:18 indicates that God's love is endless – it knows not the barriers of time as we do – it is eternal. It means that the love of God is so long it is forever. We are told in Jeremiah 31:3 that "The Lord hath appeared of old unto me, saying, yea, I have loved thee with an **everlasting love**: therefore with lovingkindness have I drawn thee," (**bold** emphasis mine). God loved us before we were ever born and He continues to love us despite our unloving natures. In Chapter 3 of this book, we learned that the definition of everlasting was, "eternal, lasting through all time." God tells us in Jeremiah that He has an eternal, lasting through all time love for us. God loves mankind with a never-ending, undying love.

God's love is a long-suffering love. The definition of the word long-suffering is, "long and patient endurance of offense" (Merriam-Webster, 2012). We have all offended God by our sins but God has a long and patient endurance of our offenses. In I Peter 3:20 the Bible says, "Which sometime were disobedient, when once the longsuffering of God **waited** in the days of Noah, while the ark was a preparing, wherein few, that is, eight souls were saved by water," (**bold** emphasis mine). This verse refers to the story of Noah in the Old Testament. Noah was told of God to build an ark or a great ship because He was going to destroy every living creature from off the face of the earth by way of a great flood. ("And God said unto Noah, The end of all flesh is come before me; for the earth is filled with violence through them; and, behold, I will destroy them with the earth," Gen. 6:13.) God told Noah that all humanity and all creatures would be destroyed, except those that would find shelter in the ark. God had seen that all mankind was wicked and evil. The ark was to be their safety from the flooding wrath of God that was to come. The Bible does not tell us, but I am sure that Noah warned the people as he was building this great ark.

This ark was not built overnight; it took some time, many years, no doubt. The people were given countless days, weeks, months and even years, to seek shelter in the ark but they refused. God was long-suffering and patient during the building of the ark. He wanted them to turn to Him and worship Him instead of serving evil and doing wickedness. When the people refused their last call, He shut Noah and his family in the ark. ("And they that went in, went in male and female of all flesh, as God had commanded him: and the Lord shut him in," Gen. 7:16.) No one could get out; no one could get in. The floodwaters came and the cry of the people went up as they drowned in their sin and the floodwaters.

We are told in Luke 17:26 and 27, "And as it was in the days of Noe (Noah), so shall it be also in the days of the Son of man. They did eat, they drank, they married wives, they were given in marriage, until the day that Noe entered into the ark, and the flood came, and destroyed them all." Just like in Noah's day, people today are wicked and sinful. Jesus is our ark of refuge in today's perilous times. He came here to offer safety and repentance of sins to those who believe in Him. Those who believe in Christ will be spared from the terrible wrath of God to come. But, sadly, just as in Noah's day, people refuse the free gift of salvation dooming their own souls and choosing to perish.

Looking again at II Peter 3:9 we are told, "The Lord is not slack concerning his promise, as some men count slackness; but is longsuffering to us-ward, not willing that any should perish, but that all should come to repentance." What promise is God talking about here? The promise is twofold. In Luke 17:28-30 we are told, "Likewise also as it was in the days of Lot; they did eat, they drank, they bought, they sold, they planted, they builded; But the same day that Lot went out of Sodom it rained fire and brimstone from heaven, and destroyed them all. Even thus shall it be in the day when the Son of man is revealed." The first promise in II Peter 3:9 is that God will destroy the earth once again, this time with fire and brimstone. God has promised to destroy the earth by fire and brimstone, just as Sodom and Gomorrah were destroyed, just as the floodwaters first destroyed the earth. God is not slack regarding His promises "as some men count slackness."

God's second promise is to patiently wait for the sinner to come to know Christ as their Savior ("but that all should come to repentance"). Abraham pleaded with the angels of God not to destroy the cities of Sodom and Gomorrah if there were righteous people within the city's walls. The only righteous people were Lot and his family, whom God drove out to escape the wrath to come. Lot was reluctant to leave and was told, "Haste thee, escape thither; for I cannot do anything till thou be come thither," (Genesis 19:22). God kept His promise and destroyed the cities but He also kept His promise to Abraham by sparing Lot and his family. Those that have not accepted Jesus as their Savior will perish in the day the earth is destroyed by fire and brimstone just as the people of Noah and Lot's day did. Jesus' love is long suffering, however, to the sinner. He is still waiting today for that one – even you – to choose Him as his/her Savior.

The length of God's love does not stop there. Remember the definition for the word "everlasting?" It means, "lasting through all time." I will add another definition here, it also means "endless, timeless, and unending." Because of Christ's crucifixion and death, we have the ability to live eternally. "Father, I will that they also, whom thou has given me, **be with me where I am**; that they may behold my glory, which thou hast given me: for thou lovedst me before the foundation of the world," (**bold** emphasis mine, John 17:24). Jesus prayed to God that we might have eternal life through Him. The love of Christ is endless, timeless and unending.

I have often used the evergreen tree to explain God's love to children. An evergreen's leaves are always green year round, even in the fall when the leaves of other trees are turning different colors. An evergreen's leaves seldom fall off either, unlike other trees that lose their leaves in the winter. God's love can be compared to an evergreen. His love is always there, year round, it never fades or falls away. We may sometimes stop loving someone when hurt by them or done wrong by them, but Christ will never cease to love us for any reason. His love for the sinner is longsuffering, waiting patiently for that one to accept Jesus as his/her Savior. His love for His children surpasses anything we could ever comprehend. "Many waters cannot quench love, neither can the floods drown it," (Song of Solomon 8:6) – this is the extent of Christ's love toward us.

Chapter 5
The Height of God's Love

Another dimension of God's love to consider is **height**. In John 14 we read of Jesus telling His disciples that He would go away after His death to prepare us a place so that we could dwell with Him there. The place He spoke of was most certainly Heaven. God loves us so much that He wants us to live with Him. But, in order for us to live there, we must first be without sin. God is a Holy God and cannot look upon sin. We are told in Romans 3:23, "For all have sinned, and come short of the glory of God."

John 3:3 and 5 tells us that unless we have a spiritual birth, we cannot see God's Kingdom, "Jesus answered and said unto him, Verily, verily, I say unto thee, Except a man be **born again**, he cannot see the kingdom of God. Jesus answered, Verily, verily, I say unto thee, Except a man be **born of water** (physical) **and of the Spirit**, (spiritual) he cannot enter into the kingdom of God," (input and **bold** emphasis mine). We must experience a spiritual birth in order to enter into God's kingdom. The only way to undergo a spiritual birth is by accepting Jesus as our Savior. He paid our sin debt to God through His shed blood and paved the way for us to enter Heaven.

When Adam and Eve ate of the Tree of Knowledge of Good and Evil in the Garden of Eden, they sinned against God. They disobeyed Him by eating of the fruit. "And the eyes of them both were opened," (Genesis 3:7). Realizing their error, "they sewed fig leaves together, and made themselves aprons," (Genesis 3:7). When God came looking for them, "Adam and his wife hid themselves from the presence of the Lord God amongst the trees of the garden," (Genesis 3:8). They knew they had sinned against Almighty God. The fig leaf coverings were not enough to cover Adam and Eve, so God made them "coats of skins, and clothed them," (Genesis 3:21). The coats were made from animals that had to sacrifice their lives in order to accommodate mankind. This was the beginning of the blood sacrifice. Just as the ram coats covered their nakedness, the blood of that ram covered their sin of disobedience. God then "drove out the man; and he placed at the east of the garden of Eden Cherubims, and a flaming sword which turned every way, to keep the way of the tree of life," (Genesis 3:24). Mankind was now separated from fellowship with His God because of his sin of disobedience.

This sacrifice of innocent animals was understood by Adam and Eve as a means of forgiveness – a blood atonement for their sins. The written commandment for blood atonement was not actually penned down until God gave the instructions to Moses when He commanded Him to erect the Tabernacle in the wilderness.

The Tabernacle was God's dwelling place here on earth. You might think of it as a church or place of worship. The Tabernacle housed such items as a wash basin, a brazen altar, a table with bread and candlesticks. It also housed the Ark of the Covenant – God's Holy Seat. All of these items were used to fulfill the atonement for the sins of Israel while in the wilderness. God wanted to dwell with, speak to, and guide His people but in order for Him to do this, a priest had to purify himself and confess his own sins then confess the sins of the people of Israel. Once the priest was sanctified, he went into a section of the Tabernacle called the Holy of Holies, where the Ark of the Covenant rested. This was God's dwelling place and His seat. It was here that the priest would sprinkle the blood sacrifice of rams and sheep before the Lord for the people. One lamb had to be slain for each household and its blood sprinkled on the altar to atone or reconcile the sins of the nation of Israel. A veil hung between the priest and the Pillar of a Cloud that rested on the Tabernacle. This Cloud Pillar was God Himself.

The veil separated mankind from God. The Lord is glorious and our fleshly eyes cannot behold Him and live ("And he said, Thou canst not see my face: for there shall no man see me, and live," Exodus 33:20). The veil was to shut man out and shut God in. "And thou shalt hang up the veil under the taches, that thou mayest bring in thither within the veil the ark of the testimony (Ark of the Covenant): and the veil shall **divide unto you between the holy place and the most holy**," (**Bold** emphasis and input mine, Exodus 26:33).

The Bible tells us in Exodus 12:37, "And the children of Israel journeyed from Rameses to Succoth, about six hundred thousand on foot that were men, beside children." Notice this total did not include women and children. It is estimated that there were well over one million people that set out on this wilderness journey through the desert. Imagine the number of lambs that were slain! Was all this bloody sacrifice necessary? Yes, absolutely! Blood is the river of life for the human body. It supplies nutrients, oxygen, and clears out carbon dioxide. It even carries antibodies and helps heal cuts and scrapes. "For the life of the flesh is in the blood: and I have given it to you upon the altar to make an atonement for your souls: for it is the blood that maketh an atonement for the soul," (Leviticus 17:11). God said He gave us the blood to apply on the altar to make atonement or restitution for our souls, for our sins.

The blood sacrifice of the Israelites was merely to cover the people's sin so they could fellowship with God. In order to *live* with God in the heights of Heaven, there had to be a cleansing of sin. Cleansing could not be done through bulls' and rams' blood. Because the sin debt was so great and the lamb sacrifice became great in number, God provided One Lamb - once and for all – The Lamb, Jesus (Hebrews 10:10-12). He was the perfect and willing sacrifice, without spot, blemish or sin. This was the requirement of the sin sacrifice within the Tabernacle (Leviticus 22:19-22) and in the Garden of Eden.

Through Christ's blood, our sins are no longer covered; they are forgiven and forgotten, washed away as if they never existed. Jesus was the perfect and absolute sacrifice – no other blood sacrifice will ever be needed. Through His forgiveness of our sins, we will be able to dwell with Him in the place in Heaven that He has gone to prepare. He tells us that He is going to give us a new body that will be able to withstand God's Glory and the glory of Heaven. He also tells us that one day He is coming back to get us and take us to be with Him. "Now this I say, brethren, that flesh and blood cannot inherit the kingdom of God;

neither doth corruption inherit incorruption. Behold, I shew you a mystery; We shall not all sleep, but we shall all be changed (a new body), In a moment, in the twinkling of an eye, at the last trump: for the trumpet shall sound, and the dead shall be raised incorruptible, and we shall be changed. For this corruptible (our flesh) must put on incorruption (heavenly body), and this mortal must put on immortality. So when this corruptible shall have put on incorruption, and this mortal shall have put on immortality, then shall be brought to pass the saying that is written, Death is swallowed up in victory," (Input mine, I Corinthians 15:50-54).

The priest was required to enter into the Tabernacle each year to make atonement for the sins of Israel. Each year a lamb was slain. Jesus died only once to pay for our sin. He was "brought as a lamb to the slaughter" (Isaiah 53:7; Acts 8:32). And "Christ **was once offered** to bear the sins of many," (**bold** emphasis mine, Hebrews 9:28). "For in that he died, **he died unto sin once**: but in that he liveth, he liveth unto God," (**bold** emphasis mine, Romans 6:10). This is how we obtain forgiveness of our sins. Just as the priest would sprinkle the blood sacrifice of the ram on the altar in the wilderness, Jesus poured His blood out on the altar in Heaven. The difference is Jesus' blood did not just cover the sins of the people – it removed them! "Neither by the blood of goats and calves, but by his own blood **he entered in once into the holy place, having obtained eternal redemption for us**," (**bold** emphasis mine, Hebrews 9:12). The priest of the Tabernacle was forever walking around the altar, sprinkling blood, and asking for forgiveness. "But this man, after he had offered one sacrifice for sins for ever, **sat down** on the right hand of God," (**bold** emphasis mine, Hebrews 10:12). Jesus was able to sit down after His Blood sacrifice was applied to the altar in Heaven! The sin atonement was never complete until the Redeemer's Blood was applied! Because of Jesus, we will be able to live with Him in Heaven.

But the height of God's love does not end there! When Jesus died on the cross, "the veil of the temple was rent in twain from the top to the bottom" (Matthew 27:51, Mark 15:38, Luke 23:45). The Temple was the fixed version of the Tabernacle in the Wilderness, which was moved from place to place. When the veil was torn, it opened the Holy of Holies to ALL. This meant that anyone could now go before God as long as they came by way of Jesus' blood. "Let us therefore come boldly unto the throne of grace (the Holy of Holies), that we may obtain mercy, and find grace to help in time of need," (Input mine, Hebrews 4:16). Some religions would have you to believe that you must speak to God through a priest just as they did in the Tabernacle in the Wilderness and in the fixed Temple. This was abolished when Jesus became mankind's sacrificial lamb on Calvary's cross. "Seeing then that we have a great high priest, **that is passed into the heavens**, Jesus the Son of God." (**bold** emphasis mine, Hebrews 4:14). Jesus became the High Priest in Heaven speaking to God on mankind's behalf. Each time we pray to God, Jesus carries our petitions to Him because "We have such an high priest, who is set on the right hand of the throne of the Majesty in the heavens; A minister of the sanctuary, and of the true tabernacle, which the Lord pitched, and not man," (Hebrews 8:1-2). "Let us therefore come boldly unto the throne of grace," (Hebrews 4:16)!

Before this time, only the priest was allowed to bring petitions to God. The people of Israel were not allowed to approach the altar to ask for forgiveness for themselves. Only the priest had that power. He was the anointed of God. This was his calling. If anyone else attempted to go before the altar and into the Holy of Holies, they would have been slain of God. But, whenever the Blood of Jesus was applied, it opened the gateway to God for all to come into His Court. "Having therefore, brethren, **boldness to enter into the holiest by the blood of Jesus**," (**bold** emphasis mine, Hebrews 10:19). And there to meet us is Jesus, girded as the priest of the Tabernacle, ready to hear our prayer and to plead our case before God. "For Christ is not entered into the holy places made with hands, *which are* the figures of the true; **but into heaven itself, now to appear in the presence of God for us**," (**bold** emphasis mine, Hebrews 9:24).

Jesus had to take on the likeness of mankind in order to be a suitable sacrifice *for* mankind. "For verily he took not on him the nature of angels; but he took on him the seed of Abraham," (Hebrews 2:16). He could not have become like one of the angels to redeem fallen man, He had to become man. In so doing, He experienced what mankind experiences – He feels what mankind feels. "For we have not an high priest **which cannot be touched with the feeling of our infirmities**; but was in all points tempted like as we are, yet without sin," (**bold** emphasis mine, Hebrews 4:15). He was tempted as all of us are tempted (read Matthew 4:1-11) with lust of the flesh, (vs. 3), with lust of the eye (vs. 5) and with the pride of life (vs. 8) – all that tempts us falls into one of these three categories. Since Jesus became man, He can relate and associate with mankind and what he goes through. Because He is begotten of God, He can communicate these things to God (Hebrews 2:9, 14-17). "For in that **he himself hath suffered** being tempted, **he is able to succour** (comfort) them that are tempted," (**bold** emphasis and input mine, Hebrews 2:18). Jesus is able to assist, comfort and relieve us because of what He suffered here on earth. "For there is one God, and **one**

mediator between God and men, the man Christ Jesus," (**bold** emphasis mine, I Timothy 2:5). "But this man (Jesus), because he continueth ever, hath an unchangeable priesthood. Wherefore he is able to save them to the uttermost that come unto God by him, seeing he ever liveth to make intercession for them. For such an high priest became us, who is holy, harmless, undefiled, separate from sinners, and made higher than the heavens; Who needeth not daily, as those high priests, to offer up sacrifice, first for his own sins, and then for the people's: for this he did once, when he offered up himself," (Hebrews 7:24-27).

Praying to God has but one requirement. Just as the Priest of the Tabernacle and Temple had to be sanctified or made pure before approaching God, we must also be pure in heart and without sin. "If I regard iniquity in my heart, the Lord will not hear me," (Psalm 66:18). The Bible warns that if we come to God with known unconfessed sin in our lives that God will not hear us; Jesus will not hear either. We must first ask for forgiveness of our sins before approaching God's throne room.

If you have never accepted Jesus as your personal Savior, the only prayer Jesus will hear of you is one of repentance. "Now we know **that God heareth not sinners**: but if any man be a worshipper of God, and doeth his will, him he heareth," (**bold** emphasis mine, John 9:31). You must have accepted Jesus as your Savior before your prayers will be heard. Your prayer must first be that of repentance (Refer to Romans 10:9, 13 and I John 1:9).

The height of God's love reaches from here to Heaven above even to God Almighty. This is all due to Christ's love for mankind. "Thanks be unto God for his unspeakable gift," (II Corinthians 9:15). Our High Priest, Jesus, relays our prayers to God. What a Savior!

Chapter 6
The Depth of God's Love

The last dimension to consider of God's love is **depth**. So deep is the Lord's love for us that He went to hell for us. Jesus "Who gave himself a ransom for all," suffered our punishment in hell (I Timothy 2:6). Jesus sacrificed His life for everybody – even for you and me. He loves one and all. This is the depth of God's love for us.

Jesus told the people that, "as Jonas (Jonah) was three days and three nights in the whale's belly; so shall the Son of Man be three days and three nights in the heart of the earth," (Matthew 12:40). Jesus was referring to the time that Jonah spent in the whale's belly after he was swallowed up for disobeying God's order to go to Nineveh and preach to the wicked people there. Instead of going to Nineveh, Jonah ran from God and boarded a ship that was going in the opposite direction.

God knew where Jonah was though, and He caused a great storm to arise, which tossed the ship and caused the men aboard to be very afraid. Jonah told the men that he was the cause of this great storm and God's wrath. He instructed the men to throw him overboard and the storm would cease. When Jonah was thrown overboard, God had a great fish waiting for him, which swallowed him. There, in the fish's belly, Jonah stayed for three days and three nights (Jonah chapter 1). Imagine being inside a whale's belly! The whale's belly would have been dark, musty and wet. The whale's stomach acid may have blistered Jonah's skin and dissipated his clothes. An overwhelming smell of dead fish may have filled the air. Each time the whale would have eaten; Jonah would have been bombarded with seawater and live, flipping fish. He may have even eaten these raw fish to curb his own hunger. He would have been surrounded by death and darkness. This is surely a picture of Hell. After Jonah repented from his sin of running from God, God caused the whale to spit Jonah up on the seashore. We can only imagine how Jonah must have looked after spending three days and three nights in a fish's belly. No doubt, he would have stunk from being in the decomposing fish that surrounded him. His skin, hair, and clothes may have been partially digested from the whale's stomach acid. In any case, he would not have been a pretty sight.

In this verse of Matthew, Jesus compared himself to Jonah – but why? Because, when Jesus died, He visited the belly of the earth – He visited Hell. We are told in Ephesians 4:9-10, "Now that he (which is Jesus) ascended, what is it but that he also descended first into the lower parts of the earth? He that descended is the same that ascended up far above all heavens, that he might fill all things," (input mine) and again in I Peter 3:19, "By which also he went and preached unto the spirits in prison." The mention of prison and the lower parts of the earth are references to Hell. The spirits in this prison are references to the Hell side where those who did not serve God or refused Him were kept. We know this because in verse 20 we are told that these spirits "sometime were disobedient." There was a Paradise side for those of the Old Testament who were loyal to God.

Everyone went to one of these places (called Hades) before Christ became a sacrifice that would allow all to be partakers of Heaven. Prior to the resurrection of Christ from the dead and His ascension into Heaven, Hades had two divisions: *Abraham's Bosom* (for those of the Old Testament loyal to God) and *Gehenna* (for the wicked dead). In Luke 16:19-27, we read of Lazarus who died and went to Abraham's bosom and a rich man who died and went to Hell. We are told that a "great gulf" was fixed between these two divisions so that no one could cross from one side to the other. The spirits were referred to as prisoners because they were separated from God. They were not allowed to be in the direct presence of God but they had the promise of a coming Messiah, Jesus, who would change all that. They believed Jesus would rescue them from Hell's prison. "Wherefore he saith, When he ascended up on high, he led captivity captive, and gave gifts unto men," (Ephesians 4:8). Isaiah prophesied that Jesus would come "to proclaim liberty to the captives," and open the "prison to them that are bound" (Isaiah 61:1). Jesus said he came "to preach deliverance to the captives" (Luke 4:18). Jesus went to Hell to preach to the imprisoned spirits held there but He also went to free them.

Jesus not only descended into Hell to free the imprisoned spirits but He also went to Hell to defeat the second death, which is the eternal separation from God. He did this by being "the first begotten of the dead" (Revelation 1:5). Just as Jonah was spit out of the whale's belly after three days, Jesus came up from Hell after being dead for three days. Jesus had the power to raise Himself from His own death because He was God. He told the people that He had the power to lay down His life **and** to take it up again (John 10:18). Because Jesus arose from the dead of His own power, He defeated the second death, the eternal separation from God. By the sacrificial shedding of His blood, He made it possible for those that had been loyal to God in the Old Testament including the saints to go to Heaven and to be in the direct presence of God. Those that accept Jesus as their Savior will also go to be in the direct presence of God when they die. Christ was the only one having the power of God to descend into Hell **and** ascend into Heaven. I Peter 3:18 proclaims, "For Christ also hath once suffered for sins, the just for the unjust, **that he might bring us to God**, being put to death in the flesh, but quickened by the Spirit," (**bold** emphasis mine). Jesus tasted death for every man. (Hebrews 2:9) This is why He is Lord over death, Hell and the grave. Jesus is "he that liveth, and was dead;" and that is "alive for evermore," and that has "the keys of hell and death," (Revelation 1:18). This can be said of no one else.

Jesus took our sin debt – the debt of the entire world – to Hell so that we as believers will never have to go to this horrible place and pay that sin debt ourselves. But He rose from that horrendous pit triumphant over death, Hell, and the grave. This is a great victory for the redeemed, for those that believe in Jesus' salvation. We will not have to endure Hell if we know Jesus as our personal Savior. Thanks to Jesus, we now have an eternal home in Heaven. God's love is so deep that it reached down into Hell for us.

In the next chapters, we will learn what it took for Jesus to pay the sin debt owed for all mankind.

Chapter 7
The Trial of Jesus

Jesus was presented for trial before being crucified. His trial was anything but fair. Judas Iscariot, one of Jesus' disciples, came to Jesus while He was in the Garden of Gethsemane praying. Judas was to reveal to the soldiers that accompanied him which man was the Christ. "Now he (Judas) that betrayed him (Jesus) gave them a sign, saying, Whomsoever I shall kiss, that same is he: hold him fast," (Input mine, Matthew 26:48). Judas kissed the door to Heaven but doomed his soul to Hell because of his unbelief in the Savior. The soldiers quickly took Jesus and carried Him away to face judgment at the hands of an angry mob.

Jesus' trial began when He was first delivered to Annas, who was father in law to Caiaphas. "Now Caiaphas was he, which gave counsel to the Jews, that it was expedient that one man should die for the people," (John 18:14). Annas served as the high priest of the Sanhedrin of the Jewish court. "The high priest then asked Jesus of his disciples, and of his doctrine. Jesus answered him, I spake openly to the world; I ever taught in the synagogue, and in the temple, whither the Jews always resort; and in secret have I said nothing," (John 18:19-20). "Now the chief priests, and elders, and all the council, sought false witness against Jesus, to put him to death," (Matthew 26:59). Jesus told them that He did not have a secret society of followers as they were implying but His ministry was always open to the public. The Sanhedrin, nevertheless, brought many false witnesses against Jesus to accuse Him of sacrilegious acts.

The high priest finally said to Jesus, "I adjure thee by the living God, that thou tell us whether thou be the Christ, the Son of God. Jesus saith unto him, Thou hast said: nevertheless I say unto you, Hereafter shall ye see the Son of man sitting on the right hand of power, and coming in the clouds of heaven," (Matthew 26:63-64; Mark 14:62; Luke 22:69). "Then said they all, Art thou then the Son of God? And he said unto them, Ye say that I am," (Luke 22:70). "Then the high priest rent his clothes, saying, He hath spoken blasphemy; what further need have we of witnesses? behold, now ye have heard his blasphemy. What think ye? They answered and said, He is guilty of death," (Matthew

26:65-66; Mark 14:63-64). They were trying to trick Jesus with words. Jesus publicly admitted to being the Son of man. Had Jesus publicly stated that He was the Son of God, the Sanhedrin and high priest would have cause to accuse Jesus of blasphemy. However, Jesus told them, "Thou hast said," indicating they had admitted who He was.

As punishment, the high priest sent Jesus to be beaten. "And when they had blindfolded him, they struck him on the face, and asked him, saying, Prophesy, who is it that smote thee?" (Luke 22:64; Mark 14:65) Jesus is all knowing and told of many things that were yet to come during His earthly ministry. Jesus could have easily named each and every person that hit Him or spit on Him. "But Jesus held his peace," (Matthew 26:63).

The Sanhedrin and high priest then sent Jesus to Pilate, who served as the Roman Governor. Pilate asked them that brought Jesus before him, "What accusation bring ye against this man? They answered and said unto him, If he were not a malefactor, we would not have delivered him up unto thee. Then said Pilate unto them, Take ye him, and judge him according to your law. The Jews therefore said unto him, It is not lawful for us to put any man to death," (John 18:29b-31). The Jews were seeking the death penalty for Jesus for blasphemy in claiming to be the Son of God. This is the reason they ushered Jesus before

Pilate. They wanted Pilate to deliver the decree of death.

Pilate was familiar with Jesus and knew of His workings. "Then Pilate entered into the judgment hall again, and called Jesus, and said unto him, Art thou the King of the Jews? Jesus answered him, Sayest thou this thing of thyself, or did others tell it thee of me? Pilate answered, Am I a Jew? Thine own nation and the chief priests have delivered thee unto me: what hast thou done? Jesus answered, My kingdom is not of this world: if my kingdom were of this world, then would my servants fight, that I should not be delivered to the Jews: but now is my kingdom not from hence. Pilate therefore said unto him, Art thou a king then? Jesus answered, Thou sayest that I am a king," (John 18:33-37a). Jesus explained to Pilate that if His kingdom was set up here on earth that His loyal subjects would have fought for His release but Jesus said that His kingdom was not of this world. Again, Jesus did not allow Himself to be accused of blasphemy by forthrightly saying, "I am a King," instead he told Pilate, "Thou sayest that I am a king."

"Then said Pilate to the chief priests and to the people, I find no fault in this man. And they were the more fierce, saying, He stirreth up the people, teaching throughout all Jewry, beginning from Galilee to this place. When Pilate heard of Galilee, he asked whether the man were a Galilaean. And as soon as he knew that he belonged unto Herod's jurisdiction, he sent him to Herod, who himself also was at Jerusalem at that time," (Luke 23:4-7). Upon learning that Jesus belonged to a different jurisdiction, Pilate then sent Jesus to be questioned of Herod.

"And when Herod saw Jesus, he was exceeding glad: for he was desirous to see him of a long season, because he had heard many things of him; and he hoped to have seen some miracle done by him. Then he questioned with him in many words; but he answered him nothing." (Luke 23:8-9) "And Herod with his men of war set him at nought, and mocked him, and arrayed him in a gorgeous robe, and sent him again to Pilate," (Luke 23:11). Here we read that Jesus said nothing as He had before. The silence of the Savior. Herod, therefore, sent Jesus back to Pilate's court for final judgment.

"And Pilate, when he had called together the chief priests and the rulers and the people, Said unto them, Ye have brought this man unto me, as one that perverteth the people: and behold, I, having examined him before you have found no fault in this man touching those things whereof ye accuse him: No, nor yet Herod: for I sent you to him; and, lo, nothing worthy of death is done unto him. I will therefore chastise him, and release him," (Luke 23:13-16). Pilate sentenced Jesus to scourging and to reprimand. "Then Pilate therefore took Jesus, and scourged (beat) him,"

(Input mine, John 19:1). The beating Jesus took was brutal.

After Jesus was sorely beaten and scourged, "Pilate therefore went forth again, and saith unto them, Behold, I bring him forth to you, that ye may know that I find no fault in him," (John 19:4). Pilate reiterated that He found Jesus innocent of the accusation brought against Him. "When the chief priests therefore and officers saw him, they cried out, saying, Crucify him, crucify him. Pilate saith unto them, Take ye him, and crucify him: for I find no fault in him," (John 19:6). Pilate then washed his hands of the whole matter, "saying, I am innocent of the blood of this just person: see ye to it," (Matthew 27:24b). At least three times, it is recorded that Pilate told the people that he found nothing worthy of crucifixion in Jesus. He told the people that Jesus did not deserve the death penalty.

Pilate even sought to release Jesus, offering to crucify a true criminal instead (John 19:12; Luke 23:25; Matthew 27:17) but the people would not consent to crucifying any one other than Jesus. Falsely accused at His trial, Jesus was taken away to be crucified at the hands of sinners.

Chapter 8
The Torment of the Savior

The book of Isaiah, chapter 53, recounts the sufferings of Christ some 700 years before His birth at Bethlehem. This prophecy remarkably explains Christ's humiliation, His rejection, and His torment at Calvary. It even gives an account of His ministry. Psalm 22 is another chapter in the Bible that describes the sufferings of the Savior many years before His appearance on earth. Jesus in the Gospels of Matthew, Mark, Luke, and John, often quotes these books and a few others. Jesus' sufferings were predicted long before He was even born into the world.

Christ's torment, however, began before ever reaching Calvary's hill and the cross. It began in a garden where He went to pray. He would often isolate Himself from His disciples and the multitudes that followed Him to pray alone. It was during these times that He spoke to God and sought comfort and guidance from Him. On the night before Jesus was crucified, He went to the Garden of Gethsemane to pray. Jesus knew what He was about to face, and He sought comfort. "And being in an agony he prayed more earnestly," (Luke 22:44a). He was so burdened over what was about to take place that, "his sweat was as it were great drops of blood falling down to the ground" (Luke 22:44b). Jesus' sweat became large drops of blood that fell to the ground in the Garden. His physical reaction was caused by His sympathetic nervous system. Jesus had agonized so much that His sympathetic nervous system invoked the "fight or flight" reaction. The sympathetic nervous system is a branch of our autonomic nervous system and is responsible for calling our bodies into action. The "fight or flight" reaction occurs as a response of the sympathetic nervous system's answer to a stressful event. It prepares our body to fight or to run. Jesus' nervous system responded to His agony to such a degree that the vessels of His sweat glands hemorrhaged (began to bleed). Because Jesus felt so much pressure over the events about to take place, the ducts of His sweat glands filled with blood, which poured out onto His skin. He knew what torture He must face, not of the cross but of the sin debt He must carry, and no doubt it troubled Him to His very soul.

After Jesus was sentenced at His trial, He was sent for scourging. Scourging was a type of cruel, inhumane beating used by the Romans that sometimes resulted in death. The victim to be scourged was usually stripped of his clothing and customarily tied to a three-foot high post with his back to the soldiers. As it is written in Isaiah 50:6, "I gave my back to the smiters, and my cheeks to them that plucked off the hair; I hid not my face from shame and spitting." Jesus gave His back to be beaten of the soldiers. A whip, often referred to as a flagrum, was used to flog or whip the victim. This was no ordinary whipping as with a leather strap or a switch. This whip consisted of a wooden handle with 3 or 4 long, leather straps attached. At the end of each strap were small pieces of bone and metal fragments. Upon the first blow, bruising would occur. Each hit thereafter would result in torn, ripped, and quivering flesh and muscle. Those glamorous pictures we have often seen drawn or painted of Jesus on a cross scarcely do Him justice. Jesus would not have looked so magnificent. He would have been bleeding. His flesh would have been ripped to shreds. Isaiah said it best when he said, "his visage was so marred more than any man" (Isaiah 52:14). It has been said Jesus would have resembled a piece of cubed steak or hamburger because of the beating He endured. Most scourgings were not more than 40 stripes, the limit a human could endure. Any more than 40 and death usually resulted.

Once the beating was finished, they put a robe of purple on Him, the emblem of royalty. They made thorns into a crown and drove them on His head with a reed ("And when they had platted a crown of thorns, they put it upon his head, and a reed in his right hand: and they bowed the knee before him, and mocked him, saying, Hail, King of the Jews! And they spit upon him, and took the reed, and smote him on the head," Matthew 27:29-30). These were no ordinary thorns like those found on a rose bush. It is possible that this thorny crown was made from a plant known as the Syrian Christ Thorn or *Ziziphusspina-christi*. The more common name for this plant is Christ's Thorn Jujube. This plant is in reality, a tree. It can be found growing all throughout the Holy Land. This tree can grow to be quite large and it lives for hundreds of years. It has fragrant, yellowish-green blooms, which flower 2-3 times per year. The Christ's Thorn Jujube produces an edible brown fruit resembling and tasting like a tart apple. At the base of each leaf are two sharp thorns, one sticks out straight like a needle, and the other is bent like an angler's hook. The Christ's Thorn Jujube's roots spread out widely and burrow deep into the soil making it hard to uproot. Its branches are said to burn brightly with great heat and little smoke. Its branches are so thickly twined that they provide plenty of shade, which is a welcome commodity in a scorching desert.

Though we are not told in the Scriptures, Jesus may have used this tree in many ways. He may have eaten of its fruit or used its branches to build a fire. During His 40 days in the desert, He may have smelled the sweet, fragrant flowers or taken shade under its canopy. He may have looked ahead in time and saw the thorns of this tree piercing His head, needle-like thorns that caused shooting pains throughout His face and head as they pierced His skin.

After being dressed in "kingly" attire, He was paraded down the streets. Scourging always resulted in tremendous blood loss. Jesus would have been weakened and near fainting from the beating. The people chanted, "And said, Hail, King of the Jews! and they smote him with their hands," as they walked Him down the streets (John 19:3). Jesus was rejected and unwanted but the worst torment and suffering had only begun.

The people wanted Jesus crucified even though Pilate and Herod found nothing worthy of death in Him. They asked that a murderer be released to them instead. Not wanting to displease the people, Pilate sentenced Jesus to death by crucifixion (Mark 15:15). Victims of crucifixion were made to carry their own patibulum to the sight where the actual crucifixion would take place. The patibulum was the crossbar, that bisector making the "T", on the pole that stood upright. A crossbar could weigh anywhere from between 75 to 125 pounds. Victims carrying this load after being flogged or whipped no doubt became faint along the way. The Bible tells us in Luke 23:26, "And as they led him away, they laid hold upon one Simon, a Cyrenian, coming out of the country, and on him they laid the cross, that he might bear it after Jesus." This was probably due to the fact that Jesus was weak from the vast loss of blood He had already suffered from the earlier beating. Jesus was so weak from hunger, thirst, blood loss, and mental anguish that He could not bear His own cross to carry it.

The victims were led through a town or on a nearby street so that all could see the condemned. A titulus (the accusation) of the condemned was written on a board and preceded them into the crowded cities. Everyone knew what the accused was guilty of. Jesus' accusation was "This is Jesus the King of the Jews" (Matthew 27:37). Upon reaching the crucifixion site, the victim was rudely forced onto the stipe, the upright post that completed the cross. His crossbar beneath, He was made ready for the nailing. Jesus willingly laid down His life for us ("As the Father knoweth me, even so know I the Father: and I lay down my life for the sheep," John 10:15). No one had to take Jesus' life from Him nor force Him to the cross.

Although Jesus was human and bled as humans do, He was still God. He could have spared His own life and body, but instead, He willingly laid down His life for all mankind. Jesus said in John 10:17-18, "Therefore doth my Father love me, because **I lay down my life**, that I might take it again. **No man taketh it from me**, but **I lay it down of myself**. I have power to lay it down, and I have power to take it again. This commandment have I received of my Father" (**bold** and <u>underline</u> emphasis mine). God granted Jesus the power to lay down His life and the power to seize it from death. "Greater love hath no man than this, that a man lay down his life for his friends," (John 15:13). Jesus said that He could lay down His life in death but that He could also raise Himself from that death. No man took His life (as in murder), but He willingly LET Himself be killed – He laid down His life for us.

The type of nails that were most likely used was not the common type of nails we use today to nail something together. These nails were long and thick and they may have resembled a slender railroad spike. There is much controversy over <u>how</u> Jesus was nailed to the cross. Some have said He was nailed through the palms but closer study has shown that the nail would have ripped through the flesh between the fingers. Another says that He was nailed through the wrists but this would go against Scripture itself ("For dogs have compassed me: the assembly of the wicked have inclosed me: they pierced **my hands and my feet**," Psalm 22:16; also in Isaiah 49:16, "Behold, I have graven thee upon the **palms of *my* hands**," **bold** emphasis mine). One hypothesis by Frederick T. Zugibe, M.D., Ph.D. and Chief Medical Examiner of Rockland County, New York, is that Jesus was nailed in the palm *and* through the wrist. He believes the nail entered in through the palm and was angled to exit the wrist on the opposite side. This hypothesis is not contrary to Scripture and would suffice in holding Jesus to the cross ("And one shall say unto him, What are these wounds in **thine hands**? Then he shall answer, Those with which I was wounded in the house of my friends," **bold** emphasis mine, Zechariah 13:6). This type of nailing (angled to exit the wrist) would have injured the median nerve in Christ's wrist. The median nerve is the main nerve that passes through a canal formed by the bones and ligaments in the wrist. This canal is known as the carpal tunnel. If you have ever suffered from carpal tunnel syndrome, then you know what kind of pain Jesus must have suffered. Severing or damaging this nerve would cause excruciating pain to be felt throughout the entire arm. The slightest movement, emotion, or even a gentle breeze would have caused unbearable pain to surge through His arms.

Once His hands were nailed down, His feet were crossed – placed one atop the other –

and a spike driven through both feet to the stipe. The nail was most likely driven through the spaces of the metatarsal bones of the ankle. This would prevent any bones from being broken. Jesus was then hoisted up and dropped violently into a hole in the ground made for the cross to stand. This dropping would reopen all the bloody wounds that had dried over. It would have driven searing pain throughout His entire body. It would have torn and splintered His flesh even more.

The nails were not what held Jesus on the cross. He could have easily called on God and a Heavenly host to rescue Him and fight any soldiers that attempted to stop Him ("Thinkest thou that I cannot now pray to my Father, and he shall presently give me more than twelve legions of angels?" Matthew 26:53). We can only imagine how God and the angels in Heaven felt on that day. I wonder if they sat on the very edge of Heaven waiting for Jesus to call on them. I wonder if they wept bitterly for Him as He suffered. I wonder if they were angered at the people. Nevertheless, Jesus said, "Father, forgive them; for they know not what they do," (Luke 23:34), as if He was calling off the army waiting for His call. Jesus' love for us was so great that He stayed on the cross and bore the shame and punishment we so rightly deserved. The onlookers mocked Jesus as He hung on the cross saying, "He saved others; himself he cannot save," (Matthew 27:42).

In John 3:14, Jesus tells His disciples, "as Moses lifted up the serpent in the wilderness, even so must the Son of man be lifted up." He was referring to the event of the fiery serpents in Numbers 21 of the Old Testament. The people had murmured against God, and as their punishment, He sent poisonous snakes to bite and kill them. When the people repented, God told Moses to make a serpent out of brass, put it on a pole, and hold it up so that all could look on it. This is the symbol of medicine today, the caduceus. He then told the people that if they looked upon the brazen serpent they would live. This was a picture of Jesus at Calvary. Just as the brazen serpent on the pole was raised so that all could see and live, Jesus was raised on a cross for all to see and live. Why did Jesus compare Himself to a serpent? "For he hath made him to be sin for us, who knew no sin," (2 Corinthians 5:21); the serpent represents sin and the pole represents the cross at Calvary. The brazen serpent saved the lives of those who looked on it and believed. Jesus hanging on the cross saves the lives of those that look to Him and believe.

Just before Jesus died, He cried, "My God, my God, why hast thou forsaken me?" (Matthew 27:46) God had turned His back on His Son Jesus. Why did God turn His back on His only begotten Son? How could He forsake Him? When Jesus sacrificed His life, He became sin for us. He took on EVERY sin of

EVERY person in the ENTIRE world. God cannot look upon sin, so He had to turn His back on His only begotten Son because of the sin He acquired. In Jesus' darkest and most needy hour, God turned away from Him. Imagine the overwhelming loneliness Jesus must have felt. He had heard the voice of His Father all of His life. He felt God's presence always. He communed with God both day and night. When Jesus cried this from the cross, He was alone, forsaken, and rejected by even God Almighty.

Victims of crucifixion could take several days to die. If the victims were still alive when a special feast day or the Sabbath day was approaching, it was customary to break the legs of those left hanging on the cross to speed up their death. When Jesus was crucified, the Passover feast was at hand. A soldier came and broke the legs of the two thieves that were on either side of Jesus. The soldier then turned to break the legs of Jesus "But when they came to Jesus, and saw that he was dead already, they brake not his legs," (John 19:33). Jesus had already died. "And Pilate marvelled if he were already dead: and calling unto him the centurion, he asked him whether he had been any while dead," (Mark 15:44). Pilate wondered how long Jesus had been dead. The soldier then, instead of breaking the legs of Jesus, thrust his spear into His side. When he did, "forthwith came there out blood and water," John 19:34b). It is believed that the soldier's spear pierced the Savior's heart. Jesus may have possibly died of a broken heart. Medical research indicates that the trauma from massive blood loss caused by being beaten, crucified, and suffering such sorrow would have caused Jesus' heart to burst. This would explain the account of blood and water pouring out when the spear cut into His side. It is probable that Jesus suffered a myocardial infarction or a rupture of the left ventricular free wall of the heart. This kind of rupture may explain Jesus' sudden death and out cry from the cross. The Bible predicted this in Psalm 69: 20, "Reproach hath **broken my heart**; and I am full of heaviness: and I looked for some to take pity, but there was none; and for comforters, but I found none," (**bold** emphasis mine). Jesus' heart quite possible burst on the cross.

At the beginning of this chapter, it was said that Jesus' sufferings, His death, and His burial had been predicted and prophesied hundreds of years before He was ever even born. Psalm 22:14-15 reads, "I am poured out like water, and all my bones are out of joint: my heart is like wax; it is melted in the midst of my bowels. My strength is dried up like a potsherd; and my tongue cleaveth to my jaws; and thou hast brought me into the dust of death." These verses describe the physical condition of Jesus' body at the time of His crucifixion. He was weak ("poured out like water", "My strength is dried up like a potsherd"). His bones were dislocated because of the weight of His own body upon the cross ("all my bones are out of joint"). He suffered from dehydration ("my tongue cleaveth to my jaws"). Psalm 22 also describes Jesus' sufferings. The very cry from the cross is recorded here, hundreds of years before it was yet uttered, "My God, my God, why hast thou forsaken me? Why art thou so far from helping me, and from the words of my roaring?" (Psalm 22:1) This was a true cry of agony – not of bodily agony, but of spiritual agony. Jesus suffered in His soul.

We read that, "All they that see me laugh me to scorn: they shoot out the lip, they shake the head, saying, He trusted on the Lord that he would deliver him: let him deliver him, seeing he delighted in him." (Psalm 22:7-8) This speaks of the sarcastic and skeptical bystanders at the crucifixion that mocked and made fun of Jesus (Matthew 27:43). Bystanders, no doubt, had seen the works of Jesus but did not believe that He was the Messiah, the Promised One. This is what truly tormented Jesus in His soul – their unbelief.

Isaiah recorded, "He was wounded for our transgressions, he was bruised for our iniquities: the chastisement of our peace was upon him; and with his stripes we are healed," (Isaiah 53:5). These verses refer to the beating and scourging of Jesus before He was crucified. He was beaten so badly that His appearance was disfigured and mangled ("his visage was so marred," Isaiah 52:14). He was bruised at the hands of the Roman soldiers when they hit Him and smote Him ("he was bruised for our iniquities").

We are told in Psalm 69:21 that, "They gave me also gall for my meat; and in my thirst they gave me vinegar to drink." This was fulfilled in Matthew 27:34 when, "They gave him vinegar to drink mingled with gall: and when he had tasted *thereof*, he would not drink." The vinegar mixed with gall was believed to have numbing properties and was offered to those who were being crucified to deaden pain.

The Psalmist in 34:20 wrote, "He keepeth all his bones: not one of them is broken," and this was fulfilled when the Roman soldier came to break the legs of those on the cross to speed up death. Jesus was dead already so the soldier did not break His legs. "For these things were done, that the scripture should be fulfilled, A bone of him shall not be broken," (John 19:36).

Zechariah wrote, "they shall look upon me whom they have pierced, and they shall mourn for him, as one mourneth for *his* only son," (Zechariah 12:10). Zechariah's prophecy was fulfilled when the Roman soldier thrust his spear into Jesus' side ("look upon me whom they have pierced").

Isaiah even prophesied Jesus' burial in the tomb. "And he made his grave with the wicked, and with the rich in his death; because he had done no violence, neither *was* any deceit in his mouth," (Isaiah 53:9).

In Ezekiel 6:9, God says that He is broken because of the nation's "whorish heart, which hath departed from me, and with their eyes, which go a whoring after their idols." The most agonizing torment of the Lord Jesus Christ is not that of the beatings nor is it that of the crucifixion on the cross but it is that of the rejection of His creation – mankind. Physical wounds will heal but the wounds of rejection remain open and inflamed. Christ gave His life that we might live but we refuse Him. This is the Savior's real torment, and it broke His heart.

Chapter 9
A Resurrected Savior

After Jesus died, Joseph of Arimathaea with the help of Nicodemus took Jesus' body from the cross. They then wrapped His body in linen and laid Him in Joseph's tomb (Matthew 27:59-60; Mark 15:43,46; Luke 23:50-53; John 19:38-42). A great stone was rolled over the door to the sepulcher (tomb or a cave-like grave) so that no one could get in (Matthew 27:60). The disciples and those that followed Him were deeply grieved at His death. They had seen His miracles of healing. They had heard His parables and teachings. They had enjoyed His companionship. Now He was gone.

Jesus warned them that this day would come. "From that time forth began Jesus to shew unto his disciples, how that he must go unto Jerusalem, and suffer many things of the elders and chief priests and scribes, and be killed" (Matthew 16:21a). This is also recorded in Mark 8:31a, Luke 9:22 and again in Luke 17:25. In each of these verses, Jesus also told His disciples and followers that He would be raised from the dead ("and be raised again the third day" Matthew 16:21b; also in Mark 8:31b and Luke 9:22b). Jesus predicted His own death, burial, and resurrection. He even told them how long He would be in the grave.

Joseph of Arimathaea and Nicodemus were very wealthy, well-to-do men. Because of Joseph's status and wealth, he was able to own a tomb in Jerusalem. This was the same tomb that Jesus was buried in ("he made his grave .... with the rich in his death"). All these things were prophesied (see Chapter 8 of this book). All these things were fulfilled. However, the disciples had either forgotten these prophecies and teachings or else they did not believe, for they mourned at the death of Jesus. They did not look for Him to return from the grave.

The Jews did not embalm or preserve bodies as the Egyptians did, but it was Jewish custom to wrap the dead bodies in linen with spices dispersed throughout. When Jesus died, it was close to the feast of the Passover. Jesus' burial was done quickly so as not to upset the feast. In so doing, they were not able to complete the burial procedure fully and only wrapped Jesus in a linen cloth and laid him in the new tomb. Joseph of Arimathaea and

Nicodemus later prepared spices and planned to finish the burial procedure the following day (Matthew 27:59, Mark 15:46a, Luke 23:53a).

After the feast day passed, Mary Magdalene and Mary, the mother of James, came to the tomb bringing those spices that they might finish the burial procedure on the body of Jesus (Matthew 28:1, Mark 16:1, Luke 24:1, John 20:1). They received a surprise! When they arrived at the tomb, the women discovered that the great stone, which blocked the entrance, had been rolled away and that Jesus was gone. Mary Magdalene swiftly ran and told Simon Peter and John that Jesus was gone. Peter and John dashed to the tomb. Stooping down, they saw the linen clothes Jesus had been wrapped in lying empty inside the tomb (John 20:2-8). At this point, the disciples and the women thought someone had stolen or moved the body of Jesus. They still had not recalled what Jesus had told them concerning His resurrection, "and the third day he shall rise again," (Matthew 20:19, Mark 10:34, Luke 18:33).

Mary stood outside weeping. Looking into the tomb, she saw two angels, one sitting at the head of the bench where Jesus was laid, and the other sitting at the foot. The angels asked Mary why she was weeping. Mary said, "Because they have taken away my Lord, and I know not where they have laid him," (John 20:13). Weeping and sorrowful, she turned to exit the tomb only to see someone standing by the door. Supposing he might know where they had taken the body of Jesus, she asked, "Sir, if thou have borne him hence, tell me where thou hast laid him, and I will take him away," (John 20:15). Mary did not realize that the man she was speaking to was Jesus – until He called her name (John 20:16).

The disciples and many others saw Jesus after His resurrection. "And he was seen many days of them which came up with him from Galilee to Jerusalem, who are his witnesses unto the people," (Acts 13:31). "To whom also he shewed himself alive after his passion by many infallible proofs, being seen of them forty days, and speaking of the things pertaining to the kingdom of God," (Acts 1:3). "He was seen of Cephas, then of the twelve ... he was seen of above five hundred brethren at once ... he was seen of James; then of the apostles," (I Corinthians 15:5-7). These things were written by witnesses that we might know that Jesus is alive and well. Jesus showed Himself to others to prove He had been resurrected.

He also came to instruct the disciples to preach the Good News of the Saving Grace of God to the world (Matthew 28:19-20, Acts 1:8). After His instruction, "when he had spoken these things, while they beheld, he was taken up; and a cloud received him out of their sight," (Acts 1:9). Jesus went away to prepare a place for you in Heaven. He tells you, "And if I go and prepare a place for you, I will come again, and receive you unto myself; that where I am, *there* ye may be also," (John 14:3). Jesus may be gone but it is temporary for He is coming back!

"Now if Christ be preached that he rose from the dead, how say some among you that there is no resurrection of the dead? But **if** there be no resurrection of the dead, **then** is Christ not risen: And **if** Christ be not risen, **then** *is* our preaching vain, and **your faith *is* also vain**," (**bold** emphasis mine, I Corinthians 15:12-14). This is the biggest "if" in the entire Word of God! If we will not believe that Jesus was truly resurrected from the grave and is alive and well, then we have no hope. We have the written testimony of many witnesses that Jesus is alive. He is our resurrected Savior. What is there to doubt?

Chapter 10
The Heartbeat of the Master

In John 13:23, we read of one of the disciples leaning on the bosom of Jesus. This disciple was Saint John, who wrote the Gospel of John and the book of the Revelation in the Bible. John referred to himself as "the disciple whom Jesus loved," not because he was bragging but quite the opposite. Saint John did not refer to himself in this way in order to make others jealous of him. He referred to himself in this manner because of his modesty and humility. Saint John so loved Jesus that he sought only to magnify Him in his Gospel writing. John used his name as little as possible in order to exalt the name of Jesus. Jesus loved John because John made Jesus the center of his life.

While the other disciples were occupied with lesser matters, John lost himself in Jesus much like Mary did while Martha was "cumbered about much serving" (Luke 10:40).

John did not leave Jesus when He was arrested; he was there in the inner chamber with him (John 18:15, 16). He did not deny Him as Peter did but was at the foot of the cross when He died (John 19:26, 27). John saw the glory of Jesus while it remained hidden from the other disciples. The disciples listened to Jesus' parables and sayings but John HEARD them with deep meaning. John knew and realized that Jesus was God in the flesh. John had no room for any other love. He was so overwhelmed by the love of Jesus that Jesus became his treasure. "For where your treasure is, there will your heart be also," (Matthew 6:21).

I have often pictured John leaning on Jesus' bosom and I am convinced that John heard the heartbeat of Jesus. What a wonderful sound that must have been! I have laid my head upon the bosom of my husband and heard his heartbeat. I was overwhelmed with feelings of warmth, love, and peace. John so loved Jesus that he desired to hear His heartbeat. He desired to be closer to the Lord. By hearing the heartbeat of Jesus, he heard the heartbeat of the Almighty God. He heard the heartbeat of a Savior that was extinguished on the cross from being so broken over sinners. Jesus' heartbeat was true and faithful. It beat with true love. Love for mankind, love that went to the cross and died so that all might live.

The book of John is written like no other. John wrote sayings that were uttered by the Master that the other Gospels did not mention. The book of the Revelation records things that were made known only to John. It was to John that the rapture of mankind from God's wrath was shown. It was to John that the Heavenly city was revealed. It was to John that the destruction of the entire world and of Satan was unveiled. Because of John's devotion to the Savior and because his heart was so fixed on Jesus, John experienced things that others could not.

The heartbeat that John heard beat for lost man. Jesus' treasure was (and still is) a lost and dying world. "Jesus hated wickedness so much that He bled to wound it to the heart; He died that it might die; He was buried that He might bury it in His tomb; and He rose that He might ever trample it beneath His feet," (C.H. Spurgeon). Pilate attempted to release Jesus but the people insisted that He be crucified. "His blood be on us, and on our children," was their cry (Matthew 27:25). Thank God! His blood is upon us and our children! Without it, we would be doomed for Hell. Caiaphas' innocent declaration was that "it was expedient that one man should die for the people" (John 18:14).

Sinner, Jesus died for you. He loves you that much. You are His treasure. He can save you from the sinful life you are living. His salvation is a free gift. You have only to accept it. Salvation is as simple as **ABC**: Admit that you are a sinner ("As it is written,

There is none righteous, no, not one," Romans 3:10; "For all have sinned, and come short of the glory of God," Romans 3:23.), **B**elieve that Jesus can save you from your sin ("For whosoever (that's you!) shall call upon the name of the Lord shall be saved," Romans 10:13.); **C**onfess that you are a sinner ("That if thou shalt confess with thy mouth the Lord Jesus, and shalt believe in thine heart that God hath raised him from the dead, thou shalt be saved," Romans 10:9.) Salvation is a simple and **free** gift. You have the promise of Jesus that He will redeem you and cleanse you from all your unrighteousness.

Christian, our treasure should be Jesus. In the book of the Revelation, we read about a church in Ephesus. This church had become so wrapped up in activities and soundness of doctrine and practice that they had gotten cold on God. They had labored, had repelled evil, had suffered for the cause of Christ, and had tried those that said they were of God. They were busy in church affairs and were recognized of God for this (Revelation 2:2-3). Nonetheless, God had something against them. They had forsaken the <u>love of God</u>. Jesus told a lawyer, "Thou shalt love the Lord thy God with all thy heart, and with all thy soul, and with all thy mind. This is the first and great commandment. And the second is like unto it, Thou shalt love thy neighbor as thyself," (Matthew 22:37-39). God should be our first love. We should love Jesus as John did – with our whole being. Nothing else should matter. Where is your treasure? Is it in worldly possessions? Or, is it in Jesus? Will God say to you as He did to the church at Ephesus, "Nevertheless I have somewhat against thee, because thou hast left thy first love?" (Revelation 2:4)

Jesus had a heartbeat for mankind. He told the lawyer that the second great commandment was to love your neighbor. Jesus was once asked, "And who is my neighbor? (Luke 10:29). Jesus' answer was the parable of the Samaritan (Luke 10:30-37). His desire was to spare mankind from the torment of Hell. This should also be our desire as saved Christians. We should yearn to see souls spared and saved. Our heartbeat should be as the Master's – one that beats for a lost and dying world.

Chapter 11
Child-Like Faith

In Matthew chapter 19 verses 13 - 15, the Bible says, "Then were there brought unto him little children, that he should put his hands on them, and pray: and the disciples rebuked them. But Jesus said, Suffer little children, and forbid them not, to come unto me: for of such is the kingdom of heaven. And he laid *his* hands on them, and departed thence."

In these verses of Scripture, Jesus was scolding the disciples because they reprimanded those that brought children to Him for Him to bless and to pray over. Those that brought the children were probably parents or grandparents that had followed Jesus' teaching and preaching and wanted His blessings on their children. Jesus saw something in the children that He did not see in adults – faith. Children are very trusting and impressionable. Who better to be impressed by than Jesus! Jesus was telling the disciples not to forbid children to come to Him. He made this reference, "for of such is the kingdom of heaven." Why would Jesus say this? Jesus compared Heaven to many things in His teachings. He often used parables and stories to teach His disciples and the multitudes that followed Him. He compared Heavenly things to familiar things of everyday life. This helped the disciples and the people to understand His teachings. Here He was comparing children to the Kingdom of Heaven.

Children will believe what you tell them. If you tell them the moon is purple, they will believe it until they learn otherwise. They will defend their belief, too. They have faith and confidence in their parents and other adults to take care of them until they are old enough to take care of themselves. Their prayers are simple and without selfishness or evil intent. Even though rebellion courses through their veins, the stern hand of a parent can subdue them. Children are not vain; they care and show concern over others. They are bold and not afraid of the unknown.

Adults are just the opposite. They have little faith in unseen things and their prayers are all too often selfish and prayed for their own gain. When an adult rebels against the law, they are not so easily subdued by "the long arm of the law" or even by God Himself. Some even repeat the same crime over and over again. Adults are sometimes vain, thinking only of their own selfish pleasures and concerns. They seldom show concern for the lost soul on the street or overseas. Adults shy away from an opportunity to witness and share the Gospel with others.

Jesus was saying that we must become as a little child - **believing, trusting, unselfish, innocent, and apt to be subdued** - before we can be a part of Heaven. We must believe in the unseen, the unheard and the un-thought of. We must have faith in the Word of God and in Jesus Christ.

When you sit down in a chair, do you stop to inspect it? Do you check to see if it is sturdy enough for you to sit in? Do you examine it carefully and move it about to see how durable it is? Of course not. No matter what chair we may sit in, we have confidence and faith in that chair to hold us up. We seldom ever give it a second thought. We could apply this to several things in our lives – our beds, the roof over our heads, a light switch. We have faith in all these things to work and to hold up, as they should. Why then can we not believe that Jesus will save us, keep us, and deliver us from our sins and from the torment of Hell? Why can we not believe that He will take care of our needs? Faith simply means believe or trust. We put our trust in many man-made things. Why can we not put our trust in Heavenly things – in Jesus? What hurt would it cause us?

Jesus tells us in the latter part of John 6:37, "and him that cometh to me I will in no wise cast out." Jesus did not turn away the little children. He welcomed them into His arms and He blessed them. Jesus did not turn away those possessed of devils, sick with leprosy, or caught in acts of adultery. He forgave them all and welcomed them as a father welcomes a child home. He will not turn us away either, no matter what age we are. Salvation through Jesus is a **free** gift – all we must do is accept it. We must believe in Jesus with the faith of a little child. We must trust Him. We must not try to comprehend it, analyze it or understand it as we adults often do with things we do not understand. We must just simply believe it.

"Now faith *is* the substance of things hoped for, the *evidence* of things not seen," (**bold** and *italic* emphasis mine, Hebrews 11:1). "But without faith *it is* impossible to please *him*: for he that cometh to God **must believe that he is**, and *that* he is a rewarder of them that diligently seek him," (**bold** emphasis mine, Heb. 11:6). Hebrews chapter 11 is often referred to as the chapter of faith. Many heroes of the faith are mentioned in this chapter. They believed in the unseen. They had only <u>a promise</u> of things to come. Unlike them we have the proof. "To whom also he shewed himself alive after his passion **by many infallible proofs**, being seen of them forty days, and speaking of the things pertaining to the kingdom of God," (**bold** emphasis mine, Acts 1:3). "And that he was seen of Cephas, then of the twelve: After that, he was seen of above five hundred brethren at once; … And last of all he was seen of me also (Paul), as of one born out of due time," (Input mine, I Corinthians 15:5-8). Jesus left us proof of His existence.

These were all witnesses to the promise of Christ's coming that was made in the Old Testament. Nevertheless, we must still become as "little children" and believe by faith. We must believe that He is real and that He saves from sins even though we have not physically seen Jesus with our own eyes. Just believe it as the Old Testament Saints did. Faith is the substance of things we hope for. Faith is the evidence of things we do not see. "These things have I written unto you that believe on the name of the Son of God; that ye may know that ye have eternal life, and that ye may believe on the name of the Son of God," (I John 5:13). Jesus wrote His love in red. Just believe!

References

King James 1611 Authorized Print of the Holy Bible

Arndt, S. (1997-2001). Ziziphus Plant, Retrieved from http://chemsrv0.pph.univie.ac.at/ska/ziplant.htm

Christian Answers.net. (1995-2012). Jesus. Retrieved from http://www.christiananswers.net/dictionary/jesus.html

Christian Answers.net. (1995-2012). Christ. Retrieved from http://christiananswers.net/dictionary/christ.html

Edwards, W., Wesley, J. G., & Hosmer, F. (2001). Study on the physical death of Jesus Christ, Retrieved from http://www.frugalsites.net/jesus/

Greene, Oliver B., The Gospel According to John, (May 1976), Introduction

Merriam-Webster, Inc. (2012). Definition of "the." Retrieved from http://www.merriam-webster.com/dictionary/the

Merriam-Webster, Inc. (2012). Definition of "love." Retrieved from http://www.merriam-webster.com/dictionary/love

Merriam-Webster, Inc. (2012). Definition of "so." Retrieved from http://www.merriam-webster.com/dictionary/so

Merriam-Webster, Inc. (2012). Definition of "beget." Retrieved from http://www.merriam-webster.com/dictionary/beget?show=0&t=135 1171623

Merriam-Webster, Inc. (2012). Definition of "procreate." Retrieved from http://www.merriam-webster.com/dictionary/procreate

Merriam-Webster, Inc. (2012). Definition of "whoever." Retrieved from http://www.merriam-webster.com/dictionary/whoever

Merriam-Webster, Inc. (2012). Definition of "whatever." Retrieved from http://www.merriam-webster.com/dictionary/whatever

Merriam-Webster, Inc. (2012). Definition of "everlasting." Retrieved from http://www.merriam-webster.com/dictionary/everlasting

Merriam-Webster, Inc. (2012). Definition of "perish." Retrieved from http://www.merriam-webster.com/dictionary/perish

Merriam-Webster, Inc. (2012). Definition of "longsuffering." Retrieved from http://www.merriam-webster.com/dictionary/longsuffering

Rose Publishing. (2006). Names of Jesus pamphlet.

Zugibee, F. (1998-2005). Turin Lecture, Retrieved from http://e-forensicmedicine.net/turin2000.htm

Zugibee, F. (1998-2005). Pierre Barbet Revisited, Reprinted from Sindon N.S., Quad. N. 8, Dec 1995, Retrieved from http://www.shroud.com/zugibee.htm